Overflowing!

Jonathan Williams

All Scripture used is from the New American Standard Bible unless otherwise noted.

Copyright © 2018 Jonathan Williams

All rights reserved.

ISBN-13:978-1983976964
ISBN-10:1983976962

CONTENTS

	Introduction	1
1	The Prayer That Almost Did Not Get Prayed	3
2	For This Reason	11
3	Every Family in Heaven and Earth	17
4	Strengthening the Inner Man	23
5	Christ Dwelling in Your Heart	29
6	Sinking Your Roots Deep into Love	39
7	It is Possible for You to Be Filled with God	47
8	Start Thinking Now About God's Love for You	51
	Paul's Prayer About God's Love	55

Introduction

The words are among the most moving in Scripture. They were penned by Paul as he was praying for people dear to his heart.

Let's take a moment and listen in. Let's hear what Paul says to God about these people. Let's hear how this man prayed for his disciples and how he would have prayed for us if we had been there. The words are Ephesians 3:14-21.

> 14 For this reason I bow my knees before the Father, 15 from whom every family in heaven and on earth derives its name, 16 that He would grant you, according to the riches of His glory, to be strengthened with power through His Spirit in the inner man, 17 so that Christ may dwell in your hearts through faith; and that you, being rooted and grounded in love, 18 may be able to comprehend with all the saints what is the breadth and length and height and depth, 19 and to know the love of Christ which surpasses knowledge, that you may be filled up to all the fullness of God. 20 Now to Him who is able to do far more abundantly beyond all that we ask or think, according to the power that works within us, 21 to Him be the glory in the church and in

> Christ Jesus to all generations forever and ever. Amen.

Don't you wish you could pray like that? Here's an encouraging word for you. You can! All of us can take the words of Scripture and use them for our prayers. God loves it when we think deeply about his word and make it our own in life and prayer. This practice has been life changing for me, and it can be life changing for you.

If you are looking for a book with lots of exciting stories about the Holy Spirit's power – this book probably isn't for you. It's not that we should be disinterested in his power. We should long to see it displayed through us. This book does something else. It probes the mind of an apostle and examines how he prayed so that we can pray like him. But if we will take the time and learn how, then watch out! The Holy Spirit will work mightily in you!

As you read the pages that follow, you will learn to pray like Paul, and something else will happen – you will be filled up with God! You will be filled with his presence and overflow with his Spirit to a world that desperately needs his love.

– *Jonathan Williams*

1 *The Prayer that Almost Did Not Get Prayed!*

Did you know that Paul's prayer almost did not get prayed? What a loss if it had not been written! When Paul was writing Ephesians, which many have said is his greatest letter, he was writing passionately about the things God has done for us in Christ. In chapter one, he talks about the mighty acts of salvation including redemption, forgiveness, adoption, our inheritance, and the gift of the Spirit. He concludes with a majestic prayer emphasizing the Lordship of Jesus over all powers, all authorities, and all names, and he prays that our eyes would open to this reality.

In chapter two, he reminds us of the terrible plight we were in. We were dead in our sin. We were enslaved to the lusts of the flesh. We were controlled by the evil one. Yet, God had mercy upon us and saved us by grace through faith. Not only did he save us and reconcile us to himself, but he also reconciled all people into one Body which Paul also called a Temple of praise to God.

Spiritual Sidetrack

What wonderful things God has done! God's works inspire Paul to pray. He is ready to pen the thoughts of his praises and petitions to the Lord. He begins chapter three with these words,

"For this reason, I ...", and he is about to say,

". . . I bow my knees before the Father," and pray.

But he doesn't get there! He breaks off his thought. He doesn't pray. Instead, he goes into detail about his ministry, telling us many interesting things.

He explains that he is a prisoner of Christ Jesus (3:1), that God gave him grace to help others (3:2), and that God revealed mysteries to him (3:3-5). He describes the mystery of Christ (3:6), reiterates that God gave him grace to preach the riches of Christ to the Gentiles (3:7-8), and then talks about God's wisdom revealed through the Church (3:9-10). These spiritual wonders were carried out in Christ, and in Christ believers can come boldly before the throne of God with their prayers (3:11-12). Such glorious truths, and it is because of these truths, Paul explains, that he can endure the trials that come his way. Paul finishes these thoughts by saying that his trials were to move people toward their glorious destiny (3:13).

You can read these details in Ephesians 3:1-13. They are full of life-giving wisdom that will nourish your soul. We can be glad that Paul delayed his prayer and revealed these wonderful insights for us to learn.

Finally, he gets back to his prayer. Thankfully he did not forget! He now will finish his sentence and write one of the most majestic prayers in Scripture, a prayer that shows how we can be filled up with God and overflow with his presence. Paul says,

"For this reason, I . . . bow my knees before the Father," and this time he prays!

The Only Epistle with Two Prayers
Ephesians 3:14-21 is Paul's second prayer in this letter. It is the only epistle with two prayers. In the

first prayer, Paul talked about the remarkable achievements of Christ which he accomplished for us. Paul prayed that God would open our eyes to the wonders of our calling, the wonders of our inheritance, and the wonders of God's mighty power toward us. He then closed his prayer by talking of the great exaltation of Christ; that he is above all powers and is head over them for us. You can read that prayer in Ephesians 1:15-23 where Paul talks about God's work *in Christ*.

But the prayer in Ephesians 3 is more personal and experiential. Paul talks about God's work *in us*. He talks about the Spirit. He talks about the love of God, and he talks about the mighty work of God *in us* to comprehend this love.

We need to pray Ephesians 1 and Ephesians 3. We need the type of prayer in Ephesians 1 where we ask God to enlighten us to see the achievements of Christ, his glorious exaltation, and our future exaltation in him. This is "big picture praying." This is vision-casting praying.

We also need the type of prayer where we ask God to be real to us, to change us on the inside, and make us stronger. We need the long-range, vision-casting prayer of Ephesians 1, and the short-range, daily experience prayer of Ephesians 3.

When we have one type of prayer and not the other, we miss the full blessing of God. Let me explain. When we have only the long-range vision of Ephesians 1, or, only the short-range experiential prayer of Ephesians 3, we miss the connection between our everyday lives and the greater goals God has for us and the Church. We need both kinds of praying – long-range, vision-casting praying and short-range, experiential praying.

When I was a young pastor, my mentors impressed me with the need to be a man of long-range vision. They did this by teaching a great truth from Proverbs 29:18,

"Where there is no vision, the people are unrestrained."

They would exhort us to be men and women of great vision, of world vision – to be men and women who ask God for great things. I am grateful for this emphasis in my life.

But life still had to be lived one day at a time, one moment at a time, one experience at a time, and I was frustrated with the inability to see how the small things of life connected with God's world-wide plan. One day, I read another verse in Proverbs that helped me – Proverbs 17:24 – which says,

> *"Wisdom is in the presence of the one who has understanding, but the eyes of a fool are on the ends of the earth."*

I loved that verse. It showed me that it was a mark of foolishness always to have one's eyes on the ends of the earth, always to be thinking about far off places and grandiose ideas. I loved it because it said a mark of maturity is to recognize the wisdom that is in front of us every day, every moment, in every experience.

I learned to hold to both verses. I learned to look for the wisdom in front of me in every moment. I also held to the importance of being a man of great vision, world vision for Christ.

This is something all of us can learn. We need to be men and women with

> ➢ a big picture of the great objectives of evangelizing the world, advancing the kingdom of God on earth, and looking

forward to the day when all things are renewed in Christ, and
➢ a small picture of what God places in front of us to accomplish each day for his glory in the world.

Connecting the two is a mark of wisdom. Paul helps us with this in the book of Ephesians. He provides two prayers that promote both – the big picture prayer in Ephesians 1 that describes what God has done *in Christ* – and the small picture, daily, experiential prayer in Ephesians 3 that describes God's work *in us*. However, I don't want to imply that the prayer of Ephesians 1 is not personal or that the prayer of Ephesians 3 is a small prayer. In Ephesians 1, Paul prays that the eyes of our heart would be enlightened. That's personal. And Ephesians 3 is glorious and packed with insights that will have far ranging consequences if we pray it regularly.

Several years ago, Bruce Wilkinson wrote a book called *The Prayer of Jabez*. It was a powerful, little book that took a relatively unknown prayer of Scripture from 1 Chronicles 4 and challenged believers to pray it consistently for a month to see what God would do. Wilkinson had his stories of blessing from this prayer, and he wanted God's people to experience them also. But this would be true of any prayer. If we take any prayer in the Bible and pray it fervently and honestly for a month – asking God to make it real for us – there will be great blessing according to the emphasis of the prayer. This is true of Paul's prayer in Ephesians 3.

I have prayed and meditated upon Ephesians 3 almost as much as any other prayer in the Bible. As we go through it, I hope you will see why I have spent so much time thinking about it and praying it. I hope you will make it your consistent prayer. It will open the door to God's love, you will be filled up with him, and you will overflow to bless others. That, after all, is the topic of this book.

It is amazing to think about. The prayer of Ephesians 3 almost did not get written! Paul started to pray it and then was sidetracked to talk about other things. What if he had never gotten back to this prayer? But he did, and we can be glad.

In the next chapter, we will begin examining the content of this prayer that shows us how to be filled up and overflow with God.

2 For This Reason

Have you ever asked someone to pray, and they replied, "I don't know what to say"? Perhaps you have been short on words to bring to our heavenly Father. I know on several occasions I have been frustrated or discouraged and told our Father, "I don't even know what to say."

But Paul rarely seemed to have that problem. Yes, on one occasion he did say, "The Spirit helps our weakness for we do not know how to pray as we should," (Romans 8:26). But usually, we find a confident man who is filled with God-glorifying and Church-inspiring words. Why is that? It is because

Paul filled his mind with the wonderful works of God.

For This Reason
When Paul wrote his prayer he said, "*For this reason* I bow my knees." Paul had something in mind that caused him to fall to his knees and pray. What was it? It was all the truths he had stated in Ephesians 1-2.

After talking about the wonders of our salvation – our redemption, adoption, inheritance, and Spirit-gift – after talking about God exalting Christ to his right hand above all powers and names, after talking about how God has rescued us from darkness, and reconciled all people, Jew and Gentile, into one glorious body and temple of praise, he was ready to pray. His mind was filled with the wonderful works of God and his humble and grateful response was to bow his knees and pray for those for whom God did these wonderful things.

Paul's example shows us that the first proper response after meditating upon God's great works is to pray. Perhaps, this is why our prayers can be so weak and infrequent. Perhaps, this is why we don't know what to say – we don't fill our minds with the glorious works of God.

I fear that the most frequent motivator for our praying is our circumstances, our needs, and our desires. Don't misunderstand. Those are legitimate motivators. We find many examples in the Bible of people in difficult situations who called upon the Lord. Christ Himself prayed because of the terrible ordeal that was ahead of him.

> *While Jesus was here on earth, he offered prayers and pleadings, with a loud cry and tears, to the one who could rescue him from death. And God heard his prayers because of his deep reverence for God.* (Hebrews 5:7 NLT)

God invites us to call upon him in the day of our trouble.

> *Make thankfulness your sacrifice to God, and keep the vows you made to the Most High. Then call on me when you are in trouble, and I will rescue you, and you will give me glory."* (Psalm 50:14-15) NLT

But all praying must eventually move beyond our needs and difficulties. Praying must consider the glorious work God has already done and wants to do right now. Praying must be about God's eternal purpose moving us forward in his plan. Paul, in thinking about all that Christ had done, and in thinking about his apostolic mission and sufferings for people, was moved to pray for them. This is why he said,

"For this reason, I bow my knees before the Father."

I Bow My Knees

Paul said he *bowed his knees*. A frequent Jewish way of praying was to stand. When Solomon prayed after the Temple was completed, he stood (I Kings 8:22). When Abraham interceded for Sodom and Gomorrah, he stood before God (Genesis 18:22ff). But often, God's people would bow and kneel (Daniel 6:10), and this posture added an earnestness to prayer. Posture is not as important as the attitude of the heart, but often, the attitude of the heart will cause a change in posture.

Usually, I sit when I pray, but sometimes I sit forward when my prayers become more earnest, and sometimes I sense a prompting in my heart to kneel before God when things are very serious. I think of the passage in Daniel 6 when Daniel knelt three times a day by his open window facing Jerusalem. He would kneel because his heart was greatly moved for his city that had been conquered and destroyed by the Babylonians. He also knew the prophecies that

God would restore his people and city and would carry forward his plans for his people. Daniel was moved by his awareness of the great eternal purpose of God, and it moved him downward to his knees before him.

What moves you to pray? How earnest is your praying before God? I hope you pray about the circumstances in your life. But I want you to pray because of the great things Christ has done and to let His great work inspire great praying. I want you to say with Paul, *"For this reason* I bow my knees before the Father," and to have the great works of God in your heart as you say those words.

Would you not agree that the Church needs great praying? Why don't we pray right now?

> "Heavenly Father, we want to be great pray-ers like Paul in Ephesians 1 and 3. We want to be great pray-ers not so that we might be known as such, but because you are a great God. You have done so much for us. Your salvation is remarkable. It is breathtaking. It is the greatest achievement in the universe. It is greater than your magnificent creation and certainly greater than anything man can devise or accomplish.

"God, there is no one like you. We praise you for all that you have done for us in Jesus Christ to bring us to yourself and to bring us to one another. Father, we pray that the Church would come to know all that you have done and would come to know your eternal plan.

"We fear that we have reduced your work to some feel-good, quick-step remedies for our problems. Move us beyond that to see your mighty work in Christ who died for us, who rose for us, and who took his seat at your right hand for us that he might reign over all and that we might one day reign with him.

"As we study this prayer, we ask for your Spirit to work mightily in our hearts to comprehend your great love. We know that we will then be filled up with you and overflow with blessing for the world.

"And we ask all these things in the name of the one who has gained our glorious salvation for us, Jesus Christ our Lord. Amen!"

3 Every Family in Heaven and Earth

Paul said, "I bow my knees before the Father, from whom every family in heaven and on earth is named." In Ephesians 3:14-15, Paul mentions *the Father* and *every family*. The Greek word for Father is *pater* and the word he uses for family is *patria*. You can see and hear the similarity. Family is the meaning of the word, *patria*, and this is a play on words by Paul to remind us that every *family* and *father* on earth derives its existence from the creator who is the Father of all.

Sometimes we forget that God is Father because he created us. We must also never forget that he wants to be Father through redemption because the created sons of God have strayed from the family of God and have been sold into slavery. The Father has provided a way for the created sons of God who are enslaved to sin and the evil one to find release and to come back into the family of God through Jesus Christ.

When Paul says every family in heaven and earth derives its name from the Father, he is making a biblical worldview statement. The idea of family comes from God. This is a crucial point to understand in our days in which we hear that there can be all kinds of families such as two daddies in this family or two mommies in that one. If the idea of family is just a creation of man, that could be true. If family is just man's idea, then we are free to make up new definitions for marriage and family.

But we hold to the conviction that the idea of family comes from God and that every family on earth derives its legitimacy from the Father above, the one before whom Paul bowed his knees as he prayed. We must walk carefully in this truth lest we be lured by our culture into dishonoring the Father in heaven, the creator of all.

Fathers, let me also say one quick word to you. Your fatherhood and your expression of it to your children should reflect the Father in heaven. You are shaping your children, and you have an opportunity to give them a picture of God. I know you are not perfect in this responsibility because I was not a perfect father and am not a perfect father today to my grown children. But I did give them a good-enough picture of the divine Father that has remained with them and influenced them to seek God. By the grace of God, you can do the same.

When Paul used this phrase about every family in heaven and on earth, he also had one family primarily in mind – God's redeemed family, some who are now in heaven and some who are still on earth. We are one family, and a day is coming when we will unite in worship and joy around the throne of God and will reign with him forever. This fits with Paul's emphasis in this letter where he has labored to explain how Jew and Gentile are one family. In 2:19 he used a family expression when he said that we are God's *household*.

A Closer Look – Four Points Paul Prayed
Yes, because of Christ, we are God's redeemed family, and this reality caused Paul to bow his knees

before the Father in heaven and to pray amazing, specific prayers for this family. Let's take a closer look at four things Paul prayed. He prayed for

- strength for the inner person,
- greater intimacy with Christ,
- comprehension of the love of God, and for
- being filled up with God.

This is our goal – to be filled up with God. But we need to see that these are not four unrelated requests. Instead, they are building blocks to construct something great in our lives. They are steps to get us to a goal. They are links in a beautiful chain. We can illustrate it like this:

(I pray that you would)

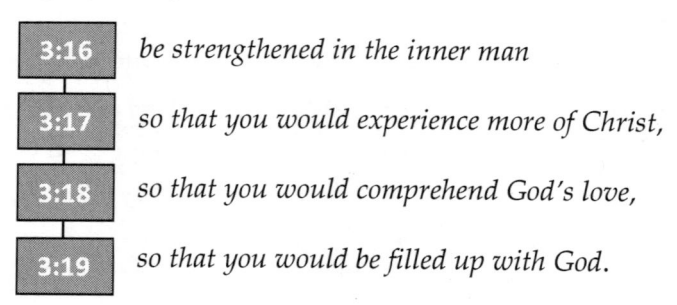

3:16 — *be strengthened in the inner man*

3:17 — *so that you would experience more of Christ,*

3:18 — *so that you would comprehend God's love,*

3:19 — *so that you would be filled up with God.*

The goal is to be filled up to the fullness of God which is stated in verse 19, but the path is through verses 16-18 – to be strengthened in the inner man (verse 16) so that we can experience more of Christ (verse 17) so that we can comprehend God's love (verse 18) and in that comprehending of God's love, we will be filled up with God (verse 19) which will then overflow to the world. Do you see how that works?

In the next chapter, we will talk about the first stage – the strengthening of our inner man.

Jonathan Williams

4 Strengthening the Inner Man

Paul prayed that we would be strengthened in our inner man. Let's look at his exact words in 3:16.

(I pray)
"that he would grant you, according to the riches of His glory, to be strengthened with power through His Spirit in the inner man."

What is our inner man? It is our human nature made in the image of God but which has been polluted, weakened, and distorted by sin. Our inner man is our will that has made wrong choices, or refused to make choices at all, or stubbornly held on to old ways. It is our intellect that has been confused by lies. It is our emotions that have been turned inside out or stifled so that we no longer feel as we should feel.

Yes, sin has distorted our inner man in many ways, but when the Spirit of God comes to us, he comes into our inner man and begins the process of changing us. It's quite a task. Sometimes I have felt sorry for the Holy Spirit. I realize that is probably a ridiculous thing to say, but when I think about the brokenness of our lives and his project to put the broken pieces together, I think, "Lord, I'm sorry for what you see at my deepest levels and the painstaking work to put me together in the right way."

But then ... that is why he is God. He is wise and able to put the broken pieces together. He does it gladly and with love because he is the faithful God who keeps his covenant promises to us.

God Reshapes Us

God reshapes our will so that we learn to surrender to Christ, to make right choices, to be pliable instead of stubborn, and to take a stand for Christ instead of being a pushover.

He reshapes our intellect so that we learn the

truth about God and life. We see the world from a biblical perspective rather than a secular perspective or a false religion. He transforms us by the renewing of our mind. Paul said it this way in Romans 12:2.

"And do not be conformed to this world, but be transformed by the renewing of your mind, so that you may prove what the will of God is, that which is good and acceptable and perfect."

He reshapes our emotions. This is a tough one because emotions are so … emotional! I sound like a dictionary definition by using the same word! But I said it that way, on purpose, because all of us have so many emotional hang ups – feeling unworthy, feeling unloved, feeling tainted, feeling dirty, or taking delight in things that are harmful to us. God must heal our damaged emotions so that we learn to feel the way God feels about things. Remember, God is a God of emotions. God experiences anger, sorrow, and joy. He created us to experience emotion just as he does.

God Strengthens Us
As God brings healing to our human nature, we find that he does more than heal, he *strengthens* the inner man. Healing is the preliminary step to get us to the

place where he can strengthen us. We are like people in a terrible auto accident. We are laid up in a hospital while our bodies heal from the trauma of the accident. Once enough healing has taken place, the hospital staff will work with us to strengthen our muscles so that we can reenter normal life.

I had my appendix taken out several years ago. The surgery took place about ten at night and the hospital staff had me up and walking the next morning! I wanted to sleep and rest and enjoy all these people waiting on me. They wanted to strengthen my body so I could check out of the hospital and free my bed for someone needier than me!

That is what God wants to do for us. He wants to get us to a normal life, the normal life he intended for us from the beginning. This normal life is only possible if we are filled up to the fullness of God. That is only possible if we comprehend his love. That is only possible if we are growing in intimacy with Christ, and that is only possible if our inner self is growing stronger. Do you see how the prayer works?

As our healing advances, God puts us through more vigorous training to strengthen our spiritual muscles. He puts us in situations that require faith. He puts us in situations that require humility. He puts us in situations where we must forgive. He puts us in situations where we must ask forgiveness. He designed these and a multitude of other lessons to stretch our spiritual muscles. The saying, "no pain, no gain," is just as true for the soul as the body.

But look at the prayer again. Paul said, I pray that God would grant this inner strengthening *according to the riches of his glory*. Warren Wiersbe, the great Bible teacher said if a millionaire gives you ten dollars he is giving out of his wealth. But if he gives you a hundred thousand dollars, he is giving to you *according to* his wealth.

God strengthens us *according to* his spiritual wealth. How does he measure it? He calls it *the riches* of his glory, and in saying this, he is pointing to the riches that he has in Christ Jesus for you. This is one of Paul's themes in Ephesians. He has spoken of

- the riches of grace (1:7; 2:7)
- the riches of his glorious inheritance (1:18)
- the riches of his mercy (2:4), and
- the riches of Christ (3:8).

Here, in 3:16, he speaks of the riches of his glory!

Christ is so rich in forgiveness that he could forgive all our sins. Christ is so rich in power that he has seated us with him in heavenly places. Christ is so rich in grace that he has infinite resources to heal and strengthen us. Remember, Paul said he preached to the Gentiles the *infinite* riches of Christ (3:8), and in this passage, he is praying according to the riches of *his glory* in Christ Jesus. How glorious is God?!

Do you feel weak? Do you feel like you have insurmountable problems? Do you have a nasty habit that you can't shake? Don't be overwhelmed by it. The Holy Spirit knows exactly what is going on and he knows the depth of the problem. His power is available to heal and strengthen you at the deepest level of who you are.

But what is the purpose of this strengthening of our inner man? That is the subject of our next chapter. It will move us one step closer to being filled up and overflowing with God.

Christ Dwelling in Your Heart

When I was around 20 years old, and getting deeper into the Word of God, I was having a Bible study with a young man who was about my age. He was trying to convince me to seek an experience to receive everything God had for me. He called it "the heavenly plentitude." I had never heard of that before, but I remember getting a funny feeling – like it was something unbiblical.

I remembered something else, it did not match what I had learned in Ephesians 3. I shared with him what I had been reading and studying in this passage – about being filled up with God. We looked at the verses together, and he didn't bring it up again!

The clear teaching of the Word of God protected me and hopefully instructed him. It is not that I did not want more blessing from God. I did! But I wanted to do proceed in my relationship with him biblically.

What does this passage say about being filled up with God? Let's listen to Paul's words again.

For this reason I bow my knees before the Father, 15 from whom every family in heaven and on earth derives its name, 16 that He would grant you, according to the riches of His glory, to be strengthened with power through His Spirit in the inner man, 17 so that Christ may dwell in your hearts through faith; and that you, being rooted and grounded in love, 18 may be able to comprehend with all the saints what is the breadth and length and height and depth, 19 and to know the love of Christ which surpasses knowledge, that you may be filled up to all the fullness of God.

There it is – the great goal all people aspire to, whether they realize it or not, to be filled up with the fullness of God. But the way Paul gets to this place of fullness is different from the way many teach. Paul does not tell us to seek a one-time experience that will fill us with God in every way for the rest of our lives.

Instead, Paul prays for a process to take place. Holy Spirit experiences are wonderful. And so is the daily relationship that God wishes to cultivate with us. When we examine Paul's prayer in Ephesians 3, we see a daily relationship and a process that takes time.

Paul has shown us that our inner man, first, must be strengthened so that, as the text says, *Christ may dwell in our hearts by faith.* Then, we will be able to comprehend the depths of his love and be filled with the fullness of God. The first step is the strengthening of our inner man, the second step is Christ indwelling us, the third step is comprehending his love, and the final step is being filled up with God.

But I Thought I Had All of God?
Let me pause, and answer a question that could be troubling you. You may be asking, "I thought when I received Christ as my Savior, I already had *all of God* in my life? If I have all of God, why do I need to pray to be filled up with God? Why does Paul pray for us to be strengthened so that Christ will then dwell in us? I thought he was already there?"

Great questions – let me answer them. Yes, if you have received Christ as your Savior, God himself has come to live within you. You don't need more of God.

You already have him completely. Many verses of Scripture teach this. In John 14:23 Jesus said,

"If anyone loves Me, he will keep My word; and My Father will love him, and We will come to him and make Our dwelling with him."

Here we see the Father and the Son coming to live in people.

When Peter preached in Jerusalem on the day of Pentecost, after he and the other believers had received the Spirit of God, he said,

"Repent, and each of you be baptized in the name of Jesus Christ for the forgiveness of your sins; and you will receive the gift of the Holy Spirit."

Here we see the Spirit of God coming to live in those who repent and place their faith in him. We definitely receive all of God. What an amazing thought – *God lives in us*! This is the reason why Christ died, rose, and was enthroned – that God might live among his people and in his people.

But again, we ask, if God already lives in us – why does Paul pray for our inner man to be strengthened *so that Christ may dwell in our hearts by faith*?

He prays this because even though *all of Christ* is in us from conversion, we don't always experience him living in us because of the weakness of our inner man and the weakness of our faith.

Who among us experiences Christ all the time? Yes, he is there all the time, but who among us can say that our walk with God, is so strong that we are always aware of him and always see his power in us and through us? I know I have not. He has always been in me in all his fullness, but I have not always walked by faith. He has always been in me in all his fullness, but my inner man has been weak in many ways – weakened by unbelief, weakened by pride, weakened by wrong desires, weakened by so many things that Christ could not express himself in and through my life with his power because my inner man was weak. And so, I have learned to pray that God would strengthen my inner man so that I may experience Christ living in me every day.

Strengthened with Power
Did you notice that Paul says, "that he would strengthen you *with power?*" Have you ever been hungry and felt faint? You just had to put something in your stomach and you couldn't wait for dinner. So, you grabbed a bag of chips and devoured them. It

filled you up, gave you a little strength, and you felt good . . . but only for a little while. Then the bad part of the chips began to take effect and you start feeling sick and shaky again! You were strengthened . . . but not with the power you would have received if you had waited for a nutritious meal.

My son drank one of those advertised 5-hour power drinks. He said it was great for five hours, but what the advertisers did not mention was what happened during the sixth hour! He came crashing down.

We know the difference between being strengthened, temporarily, with junk food and junk drink, and being strengthened with good nutrition for a healthy life. In the same way, Paul prays that we would be strengthened *with power* in the inner man. This strengthening comes when we partake of the healthy food and drink of the Spirit who empowers us for a healthy spiritual life. This healthy food and drink comes from focusing on what Christ has done for us. This is what Paul patiently taught in the first three chapters of his letter to the Ephesians. This is the steady diet of spiritual food in which we must partake regularly to gain spiritual strength.

Empowering takes time. Like an athlete building himself up to compete, it takes time for our inner man, our inner self to become strong. Because our inner man is weak, the Holy Spirit works in us to strengthen us at the core of who we are. As we grow in strength, we experience more of Christ in our life.

Does this make sense? It is not receiving more of God. It is God receiving more of us as we cleanse ourselves from sin and from the spiritual, emotional, and intellectual junk foods of life.

As God gets more of us, as we yield more areas to him, as we let him strengthen our character and our faith, we will find ourselves experiencing more of him. He who lives in us already, will dwell in our hearts – our daily experience – by faith as we trust and obey him.

Imagine God as a long-distance runner. He invites us to run with him through the adventures of life. But we are out of shape and can run only a block or two with him. He says, "That's OK. Let's start there."

He works with us, trains us, and build us up so that we can jog with him one mile, two miles, five miles, ten miles and so on. Finally, one day he says,

"I think you are ready, let's run a marathon together," and off we go with the Lord experiencing the thrill of running the race with Christ.

But we can only do this as we let him condition and prepare us for this kind of life. This is what Paul is praying in these verses when he speaks of the strengthening of the inner man so that we will experience Christ.

Did you notice, also, that he says, "so that Christ will dwell in your hearts *by faith*?" We must trust God to do this in our lives. We must trust that God knows what he is doing when he is putting us through a strengthening program. We must trust that when he died on the cross and rose 2000 years ago, he did it for us. We must trust that he has given us a new identity, a new purpose, and a new destiny. If we do not trust him in these areas and more, we will keep ourselves in a weakened condition. But if we walk by faith in his promises and in the belief that he has our best in mind, we will grow stronger and Christ will manifest himself in our hearts by the faith we exercise in him daily.

What the Church Needs

Would you not agree that this is what the Church

needs? It needs Christians who have strong inner character with strong faith. When God's people are this way, Christ's presence will be known in them and through them. What the world needs to see and hear is Christ Jesus. He is the Lord. He is the Savior of the world. The world needs to see Christ in us.

I ask you – are you ready to run the race with Christ? Are you ready to let him work on your inner man? Are you ready to stop resisting his work in your heart? Do you have areas you can identify where you need to give him control? Give those areas to him. Let Christ dwell in that part of your heart.

Many years ago, Robert Boyd Munger wrote a small pamphlet called, *My Heart, Christ's Home*. It pictures Christ coming into the home of our heart in conversion. But as he lives in us, we sometimes shut off rooms from him. Maybe we let him into the dining room, but we do not let him into the family room. Do we let him into our bedroom? Do we let him look in our attic, our closets, and our basement?

Do we lock off some rooms saying, "Lord, you can go this far, and no further"? Christ wants to be at home in every part of our heart as we trust him. When we do trust him, he will cleanse and indwell every part of our home – every part of our life.

Let's pray about this.

> "Father, this is a key area for a lot of us. We get stuck here. We have all of you, but are we willing to let you walk through every room in our heart and clean out what needs to be cleaned out, heal what needs to be healed, and strengthen what needs to be strengthened?
>
> "I pray that you would strengthen our faith – that we would trust that you want the best for us, and we would not be afraid to let you have all of us. Grant a strengthening of faith against all things that harm us – shame, feelings of inadequacy, and any fears that may control our heart.
>
> "Grant us strength by your Spirit in our inner man that by faith Christ may dwell in power in us."

6 Sinking Your Roots Deep into Love

When Christ dwells in every part of us by faith, then we are ready for the breakthrough of love. Paul prayed for a strengthening of our inner person by the power of the Spirit according to the riches of God's glory so that we would experience Christ in every area of our lives by faith.

When we get this far in our prayer – and I don't mean just saying the words – but when we get this far with God and allow him access to every part of our heart, then we will move to the most glorious part of the prayer: experiencing his love, being filled with the fullness of God, and overflowing with that love to others.

Remember – this is the goal – to be filled up with God. We already *have* all of God, but we don't *experience* all of God. We must grow up to experience all of him, and the way to grow up is by letting him dwell in every part of our hearts as we trust him. When we do this, the final steps of Paul's prayer will become real. Let's look at the steps again, but I want to return to the beginning of the prayer to set the background for the emphasis of this chapter.

> [14] For this reason I bow my knees before the Father, [15] from whom every family in heaven and on earth derives its name, [16] that He would grant you, according to the riches of His glory, to be strengthened with power through His Spirit in the inner man, [17] so that Christ may dwell in your hearts through faith; *and that you, being rooted and grounded in love, [18] may be able to comprehend with all the saints what is the breadth and length and height and depth, [19] and to know the love of Christ which surpasses knowledge, that you may be filled up to all the fullness of God.*

Paul shows us that the way to experience the fullness of God, as much as we can before we receive our resurrection body when Christ returns, is by experiencing the love of God. This sounds almost trite. This sounds almost unexciting.

I must confess, many years ago when I read this prayer, I was disappointed. I wanted Paul to talk about great experiences of the Spirit of God. I wanted him to talk about miraculous powers. I wanted him to talk about doing mighty things for God. But he didn't. He talked about experiencing the love of God. I guess that was my immaturity and fleshliness coming through. I wanted power! I wanted Holy Spirit experiences! I wanted to be a mighty man of God . . . I . . . I . . .I. But God showed me it was not about "I". It was about his love.

I learned something else. Being filled with the love of God was an experience of the Spirit. It was a miraculous event, it was a mighty work of God! God had to show me that the greatest expression of power was *to change my life so that I would be a man who learned how to receive his love and who learned how to give his love*. It wasn't miraculous powers or amazing preaching that proved I was filled up with God, it was love!

Four Things About Love

Paul says four things about love in this passage. First, he prays that we would be *rooted* in God's love. This is an expression from the world of agriculture. Paul is drawing on the rich tradition of the Old Testament that spoke of God planting his people in the Holy Land. Listen to these words from Psalm 80:8-11.

> *[8] You removed a vine from Egypt; You drove out the nations and planted it. [9] You cleared the ground before it, and it took deep root and filled the land. [10] The mountains were covered with its shadow, and the cedars of God with its boughs. [11] It was sending out its branches to the sea and its shoots to the River.*

Did you catch the phrases "planted" and "deep root"? This is the image Paul is using in his prayer. But instead of saying, "I want you to be rooted in some geographical location," he said, "I want you to be rooted *in love.*"

When we go back to Psalm 80, we find that when Israel was rooted in the land it became so enormous that it covered mountains with its shadow and even surpassed the cedar trees with its boughs. It went as far as the Euphrates River and the Mediterranean Sea. That is an amazing accomplishment for *a vine*.

This imagery points to supernatural growth that comes from God. The writer of the psalm uses hyperbole to express the supernatural work of God. Paul uses this image to speak of the supernatural growth that can take place in our lives when our roots go deep into God's love for us.

The question is – where are our roots? Are we sinking them deep into the fertile soil of God's love for us? Or, do we let them grow in other places – places of sin, places of pride, places of unbelief, places of questioning God's love? God wants to plant you and make you a beautiful, large vine that will bear much fruit, fill the land, and give refreshment to others.

Second, Paul uses a metaphor from the building industry. He says, "I pray that you would be *grounded* in love." When Paul used building metaphors, the building that was uppermost in his mind was the Temple in Jerusalem.

The Temple was a wonder of the world. It was said, "He who has not seen the Temple has not seen a glorious building in his life." Although the Jews rebuilt it under the direction of Zerubbabel after they returned from exile in Babylon, it was the work of

Herod the Great that made it a wonder of the world. It was originally intended to be 1600 feet wide by 900 feet long and nine stories high with walls 16 feet thick. To do this required a massive foundation. Builders built a trench around the entire mountain and put huge stone bricks in place for the foundation. Most of these weighed 28 tons, but some were over 100 tons, and the largest was between 560 and 630 tons! That is a foundation!

Do you want to grow and have your life be a mighty edifice for the Lord? If so, you must first dig down to go up. You must let the Lord dig deep into your heart, clear out the rubble of the old life, the old ways, the old sins and let him lay solid foundation stones of his love.

Paul said, "I pray that you would be grounded in God's love for you." When that happens, then he can make you into a temple of praise for himself. He will dwell in you in new ways and fill you up with his fullness just as he filled Solomon's temple with his glory.

Third, Paul says: "I pray that you would be able to comprehend with all the saints what is the breadth and length and height and depth" of that love. We live in a three-dimensional world. Paul speaks of four dimensions – the width, the length, the height, and the depth. When we look at a house we see it in three dimensions. We see its width. We see its length. We see its height. But we normally do not see its depth for that is beyond our vision. We are aware of three dimensions. Paul prays that we would experience four dimensions of God's love. Once again, we have a supernatural element. The vine covered the whole land, was bigger than the mountains and the trees. The building was enormously large with foundation stones of incalculable weight. Even though we live in a three-dimensional world, Paul wants us to experience four dimensions – how wide, how long, how high, and how deep God's love is for us.

Are you getting the impression that Paul wants us to know how much God loves us? Are you getting the idea that God's love for us is greater than any love we could experience in the world? Paul prays that we would be overwhelmed with love – not overwhelmed with projects, not overwhelmed with things to do, not overwhelmed with stress but overwhelmed with God's love.

But he isn't finished. After praying about the four dimensions of love, he prays that we would come to know the love of Christ that *surpasses knowledge*. This is the fourth part of the prayer. God's love is so great that we cannot humanly comprehend it – like a four-dimensional figure for us who live in a three-dimensional world.

God's love is like standing at the base of a mountain with roots that sink into the depths of the earth. The mountain is so wide we cannot walk around it and its peak so high we can never reach its summit. But, he invites us to start climbing and experience love every step of the way.

When we see that God loves us this much, and that he wishes us to experience it; and when we say "yes" to the adventure of knowing such love, then we will be filled with the fullness of God. But it all comes from God overwhelming our finite minds and hearts with his infinite love.

Are you ready to let God do this in your life? Are you ready to climb the summits of infinite love? Start by asking the Spirit of God to strengthen your inner person. Remember, mountain climbers must have a strong capacity to take in oxygen. They must train. God is training you, empowering your inner man, so that you can climb to the heights of his love.

7 It Is Possible for You to Be Filled Up with God!

Some might have read this small book and said, "That sounds nice, but it is impossible for me. I have too much sin." Or, "I have too much doubt." Or, "I have had too many bad experiences and have too much pain."

Would you read the last two verses of Paul's prayer?

> "[20] *Now to Him who is able to do far more abundantly beyond all that we ask or think, according to the power that works within us,* [21] *to Him be the glory in the church and in Christ Jesus to all generations forever and ever. Amen.*

There he goes again! There goes Paul with his extreme statements – *far more, abundantly, beyond all that we ask or think*. Don't you love him for that! God can do *far more abundantly beyond* all that we ask and all that we think.

What have you *asked* God to do? He wants to do that *and more*!

What have you *imagined* God to do for you? He wants to do that *and more*!

Paul is challenging us to ask God for the strength to scale the heights of his love. Paul is challenging us to imagine ourselves in a place of indescribable peace and joy, a place where we experience such love that the pain, the hurt, the sin, and the pride and unbelief have disappeared. Then, after we have imagined ourselves in such a place he says, "God can do more than what you ask or even imagine!"

Then, Paul says that God does it *according to the power that is already at work within us*.

Did you catch that? This power to fill us up to overflowing is *already working in us*. This is not some alien power that we attain to after years of spiritual discipline. This power is at work in us *right now*. The

Holy Spirit is inside us *right now* working on us, conditioning us, and moving us to start scaling these heights of love. God wants us to realize that he has already started this work, and he wants us to cooperate fully with him.

As Paul realized the great, sovereign love of God, it moved him to worship,

"To this God be glory in the church."

Glorifying God is not some abstract theological principle. Paul is talking about God being glorified as he works *in you* as you experience his love. This is what glorifies him. Paul then says,

"To God be glory in Christ Jesus."

God is glorified by what Christ has done in dying, rising, and being enthroned. And he is glorified by what Christ does *for you now*!

We End Where We Started

Thus, we finish where we began, by recognizing the two kinds of prayers Paul prayed in Ephesians. In chapter 1 he prayed about God's great work *in Christ*. In chapter 3, he prayed about God's great work *in us*. And he finishes the prayer in Ephesians 3 by speaking of God being glorified *in Christ* and *in us*!

Yes, to him be glory in the Church and in Christ Jesus to all generations, forever and ever. God has already glorified himself through his great work in Christ. He now awaits to glorify himself through you!

8 Start Thinking About God's Love For You!

Don't wait to put these truths into practice. Start scaling the heights of his love today by letting God's Word change you.

Go deep in thinking about all that Christ has done for you. As I have been saying in this book, Ephesians 1:1-3:13 is about God's great work in Christ. Many other passages focus on what he has done such as Romans 1-8, Colossians 1-2, and Philippians 2:5-11. Read them, memorize key sections, go over them again and again in your mind and grow in your awareness of what Christ has done for you.

But also, grow in your awareness of how much he loves you, which is the theme of this book. With this in mind, I have listed six passages. Many more are waiting for you to discover. But start here. Read them. Memorize them. Think about them throughout the day. Grow in your experience of God's love and be filled up with him!

John 16:27 For the Father Himself loves you, because you have loved Me and have believed that I came forth from the Father. (NASB)

Romans 5:5 And this hope will not lead to disappointment. For we know how dearly God loves us, because he has given us the Holy Spirit to fill our hearts with his love. (NLT)

Romans 8:35-39 ³⁵ Can anything ever separate us from Christ's love? Does it mean he no longer loves us if we have trouble or calamity, or are persecuted, or hungry, or destitute, or in danger, or threatened with death? ³⁶ (As the Scriptures say, "For your sake we are killed every day; we are being slaughtered like sheep.") ³⁷ No, despite all these things, overwhelming victory is ours through Christ, who loved us. ³⁸ And I am convinced that nothing can ever separate us from God's love. Neither death nor life, neither angels nor demons, neither our fears for today nor our worries about tomorrow—not even the powers of hell can separate us from God's love. ³⁹ No power in the sky above or in the earth below—indeed, nothing in all creation will ever be able to separate us from the love of God that is revealed in Christ Jesus our Lord. (NLT)

2 Thessalonians 2:16-17 ¹⁶ Now may our Lord Jesus Christ himself and God our Father, who loved us and by his grace gave us eternal comfort and a wonderful hope, ¹⁷ comfort you and strengthen you in every good thing you do and say. (NLT)

Galatians 2:20 I have been crucified with Christ; and it is no longer I who live, but Christ lives in me; and the life which I now live in the flesh I live by faith in the Son of God, who loved me and gave Himself up for me. (NASB)

1 John 3:1 See what great love the Father has lavished on us, that we should be called children of God! And that is what we are! The reason the world does not know us is that it did not know him. (NIV)

Jonathan Williams

Paul's Prayer About God's Love in Ephesians 3 is Part of a Greater Story

The love of God is the most important topic any of us can study and experience. God's love is not just a feeling; it is a story that has been unfolding throughout history. It is composed of six great acts. Four have taken place. We are now in Act 5. Learn about this great story of God's love.

Act 1 – Creation
Act 2 – Catastrophe
Act 3 – Covenants
Act 4 – Christ
Act 5 – Commission
Act 6 – Consummation

Act 1 – Creation tells about the Creator. He is the all-powerful God. He is One. No other God exists. He makes all things to express his majesty and beauty including humanity. Humanity is the pinnacle of his creation. God made man and woman in his image to reflect his character. They are to be creative in their fulfilling of the amazing destiny he gives them – to manage and rule the earth for his glory and for the good of all mankind.[1]

Act 2 – Catastrophe introduces sadness into the Story. Something goes terribly wrong in Paradise. The man and woman turn away from the Creator. In an unthinkable act, they rebel against God and seek to establish their own authority. They introduce sin into the world, and its consequences – suffering, sorrow, and death – follow close behind. As they bear children and their children multiply throughout the earth, the consequences of the rebellion cannot be shaken, and those consequences spread to all mankind.[2]

Act 3 – Covenants introduces a key figure in the drama. His name is Abraham. The Creator makes a covenant with him and promises blessings climaxing in the greatest blessing – through Abraham's descendants One will come who will rescue humanity from its rebellion and death. The descendants of Abraham become the nation, Israel. Israel is a light in the dark world. It exists to point the

---

[1] Read about this in Genesis 1-2.
[2] Read about this in Genesis 3-11.

nations to the true God – the Creator of the universe. But Israel fails in its mission. It becomes like the other rebellious nations of the world and must be judged. Israel's prophets tell of this judgment, but they also tell of One who will come and restore the nation to its purpose and bring restoration to all mankind. He will bring salvation to the ends of the earth.[3]

Act 4 – Christ is the turning point in the Story. The Promised One comes! His name is Jesus. He takes the Story to a new and dramatic level. He lives among his people with humility and grace. He heals the sick, gives sight to the blind, and raises the dead. He sets free the oppressed, forgives sin, and tells stories of God's great love. Not everyone is happy with his mission. The political authorities are threatened. The religious authorities are suspicious and cannot condone his mission because it does not match their ideas of what the Deliverer will do. They conspire to arrest and try him. They crucify him for the crimes of blasphemy and revolution. Three days later, he rises from the dead, gathers his followers,

---

[3] Read about **the covenant with Abraham** in Genesis 12 and 15. You can find his entire story in Genesis 12-25. Read about **the covenant with Israel** in Exodus 19-20. You can read Israel's story in the Old Testament, Exodus through Malachi.

and prepares them for Act 5.[4]

Act 5 – Commission is when the resurrected Jesus commands his followers to go into the world to tell everyone the good news. The promise that God made to Abraham – that he would bless the entire world – will now come to pass because Jesus, the Promised One, has come. He lived among us. He died for our sins. He rose from the dead and is enthroned as the Lord of all. He gives his Spirit to empower his people to spread the joyful news that God will forgive all our sins. God and humanity can be reconciled. The original destiny God gave mankind, to display his image and to rule the world for his glory, can now be restored.[5]

This good news has now come to you! What will you do with it? The most famous verse in the Bible, John 3:16, says:

For God so loved the world that he gave his only

---

[4] Read about Jesus in the Gospels of the New Testament – Matthew, Mark, Luke, and John.

[5] You can find the Great Commission in these verses: Matthew 28:18-20; Mark 16:15-16; Luke 24:44-49; John 20:21; and Acts 1:8. You can read about the first efforts to proclaim the good news in the world in the Book of Acts.

begotten Son, that whoever believes in him shall not perish but have eternal life.

Act 6 – Consummation is when Jesus returns and judges the world. Every person will give an account for his life. Every knee will bow and confess that Jesus is Lord of all and the only Savior of the world. Those who receive him will enter eternal life. Those who do not will be separated from his love. The great goal of God's creation is for all rebellion to cease, for God to display his glorious kindness in the world, and for all things to be made new.[6]

God wants every person to receive his love and to be part of the Greater Story. He also wants every person to bring the good news to others. Have you received this life-restoring message and become part of the Story? Are you telling it to others?

We would like to hear from you and encourage you. If you have received Christ as your Savior or if you have taken a significant step to become involved in God's Greater Story, write and tell us your story.

---

[6] You can read a quick overview of the end in 1 Corinthians 15:20-28 and Revelation 20-22.

You can write us at:
WGS Ministries
PO Box 90047
San Antonio, TX 78209

We look forward to hearing from you! Reach us on the web at www.WGSministries.org, email us at info@WGSministries.org, or call us at 210.717.6617

About Jonathan Williams

Jonathan pastored for over 35 years and is now the president of Word of God, Speak – a teaching ministry that advances life change, builds a biblical worldview, and connects people to God's story of love for the world. He is the Bible teacher for the historic *Heaven & Home Hour* program, *Word of God, Speak* and the creator of and storyteller for the epic *Stories of the Master* program which retells the story of Jesus and the stories he told bringing in historical and cultural details which modern people often miss, but details which make the stories come alive.

Jonathan was married to his first wife, Dee for 27 years. She is now with the Lord. They had three children and now have five grandchildren. Jonathan lives in San Antonio, Texas with his wife Kathleen, his co-worker and best friend.

For more information contact WGS Ministries at:
WGS ♦ PO Box 90047 ♦ San Antonio, TX 78209.
Email: info@WGSministries.org
www.WGSministries.org
1.210.717.6617

Also by Jonathan Williams

The Women Jesus Loved – Taking ten stories from the Stories of the Master program where Jesus interacted with women, The Women Jesus Loved dramatically presents the liberating love of Jesus to women in his time. This book shows the difference between Christ and every other person in the treatment of women and is crucial for the time in which we live where people are becoming aware of the plight of women in the world who suffer simply because they are women and vulnerable. Each chapter in this book contains questions for personal reflection or small group study.

The Prodigal Son and His Prodigal Father – Most people have heard of the prodigal son, but who was the prodigal father? In this retelling of Jesus' timeless tale, Jonathan Williams reveals who the true prodigal in the story is, explains why forgiveness can be such a hard gift to give, and how you can experience forgiveness in all its dimensions. The rich cultural and historical insights from the first century make the story come alive for readers today.

The Prodigal Son and His Prodigal Father can also be ordered in Spanish and Mandarin.

You can order these and all his books by calling 1.210.717.6617 or by ordering online at www.WGSministries.org/Shop.

Stories of the Master

Stories of the Master is Jonathan's storytelling program. He incorporates historical and cultural details from the works of scholars such as Dr. Kenneth Bailey and Gary Burge. Dr. Bailey spent 40 years living and teaching New Testament in Egypt, Lebanon, Jerusalem, and Cyprus. He is the emeritus research professor of Middle Eastern New Testament studies for the Tantur Ecumenical Institute in Jerusalem and is the author of many enlightening works including *Jesus Through Middle Eastern Eyes*. Dr. Gary Burge is professor of New Testament at Wheaton College and the author of numerous books including *Jesus: The Middle Eastern Storyteller*.

Stories of the Master is heard worldwide on Trans World Radio and in Albania, Kosovo, and Nepal in their native languages. You can hear all the stories at www.StoriesoftheMaster.com. The goal of this storytelling program is to introduce people to Jesus of Nazareth. The events in his life and the stories he told are among the most famous in the world. It is our belief and hope that as people hear of Jesus, his power over sickness, evil spirits, sin, and death, they will be attracted to him and want to learn more about his mission to establish the kingdom of God and his vision for the world.

You can bring Jonathan to your church to hear these stories live. People have always loved stories. It's time for the world to hear again, *The Stories of the Master*! Contact him at PO Box 90047 – San Antonio, TX 78209 or call 1.210.717.6617.

Made in the USA
Columbia, SC
27 February 2018